BRAZIL
WORLD ADVENTURES

BY GEMMA MCMULLEN

BookLife

©This edition was
published in 2017.
First published in 2016.

Book Life
King's Lynn
Norfolk PE30 4LS

ISBN: 978-1-910512-62-3

Written by:
Gemma McMullen

Edited by:
Harriet Brundle

Designed by:
Ian McMullen

A catalogue record for this book
is available from the British Library.

BRAZIL
WORLD ADVENTURES

CONTENTS

Words that look like **this** can be found in the glossary on page 24.

WHERE IS BRAZIL?

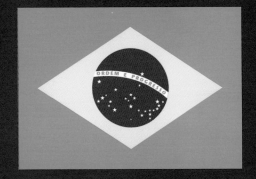

BRAZIL

Brazil is located in South America. It is the largest country in South America. The capital city of Brazil is called Brasília.

Brazil has a very large **population**. Only four other countries in the world have more people living in them than Brazil.

WEATHER AND LANDSCAPE

The weather is nearly always warm in Brazil.
The warmest months in Brazil are usually January,
February and March.

Over half of Brazil is covered by tropical rainforests, which are very wet. Other parts of Brazil are very dry and covered in deserts.

TROPICAL RAINFOREST

DESERT

CLOTHING

The **traditional** style of clothing in Brazil is different from place to place. Many styles of clothing in Brazil are comfortable and colourful.

COMFORTABLE & COLOURFUL

In the countryside, many Brazilians wear traditional head scarves. In the cities, the clothing is more **modern**.

HEAD SCARF

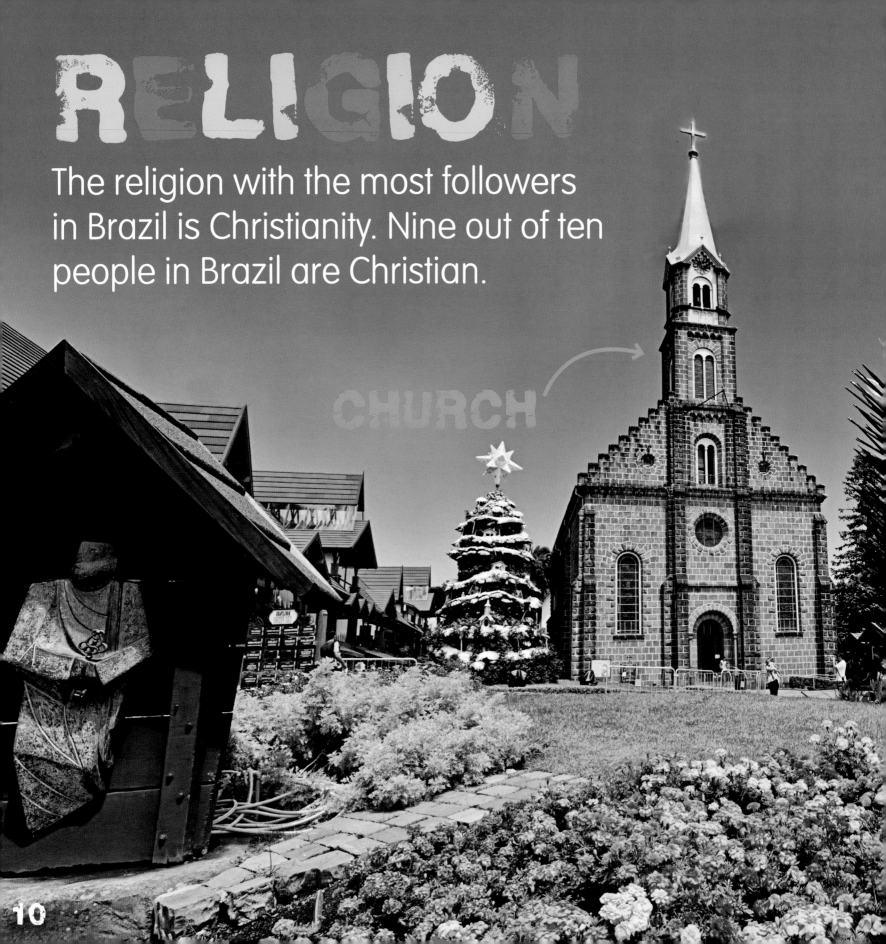

RELIGION

The religion with the most followers in Brazil is Christianity. Nine out of ten people in Brazil are Christian.

CHURCH

People from all over the world visit the statue every day.

Christ the Redeemer is a huge statue in Brazil and many people travel to Brazil to see it.

FOOD

Feijoada is a popular dish in Brazil. It is a stew made from pork and black beans.

FEIJOADA

Brazil is also known for its barbecue food. People often barbecue meat and vegetables at home. A special piece of beef called picanha is very popular in Brazil.

AT SCHOOL

Children in Brazil usually start school at the age of five and usually stay at school until they are fourteen. Children often start school at 7 o'clock in the morning.

There are after school clubs in Brazil where children can play sports and music.

AT HOME

Many Brazilians who live in towns or cities live in flats. At home, children often like to play games and watch television in their free time.

FLATS

Some parts of Brazil are **surrounded** by rainforests and are very hard to get to. The people that live there do not leave very often.

FAMILIES

Most children in Brazil live with their parents and **siblings**. People often try to live close to their grandparents, aunts and uncles.

In most Brazilian families, the parents go to work. In some families, one parent stays at home to look after the house and the children.

SPORT

Football
is the most
popular sport
in Brazil. Brazil's
football team have
won the World Cup
many times.

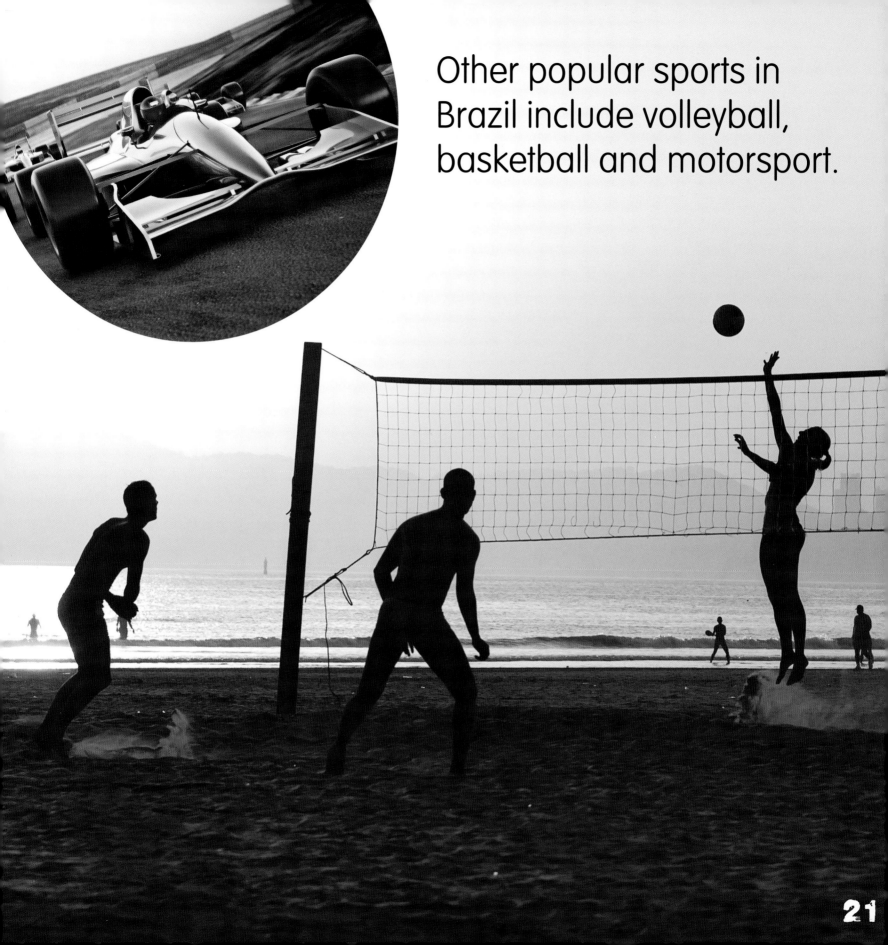

Other popular sports in Brazil include volleyball, basketball and motorsport.

FUN FACTS

PUMA

ARMADILLO

TAPIR

Brazil is home to many amazing animals, including armadillos, pumas and tapirs.

There are over 4,000 airports in Brazil.

The Amazon River is in Brazil. It is the second longest river in the world.

GLOSSARY

modern   something from recent or present times

population   the number of people living in a place

siblings   brothers and sisters

surrounded   covered on every side

traditional   ways of behaving that have been done for a long time

INDEX